What's in this book

This book belongs to

_____

T0351526

神奇的笔 The magic pen

学习内容 Contents

沟通 Communication

说出文具名称
Say the names of some
stationery items

背景介绍：
浩浩和爸爸一起看《神笔马良》的故事。故事的主角是一个叫马良的爱画画的男孩。马良有一支神笔，用这支笔画的东西都会变成真的。他用这支笔帮助了很多人，并惩罚了坏人。图中书上展现的是马良画了一只白鹤，结果白鹤就扇着翅膀飞走的情景。

生词 New words

☆	也	also, as well
☆	纸	paper
☆	笔	pen
☆	铅笔	pencil
☆	橡皮	rubber
☆	尺子	ruler
☆	本子	notebook
☆	文具盒	pencil case
☆	用	to use
☆	恐龙	dinosaur

句式 Sentence patterns

我也有一支神奇的笔。
I also have a magic pen.

浩浩也笑着说。
Hao Hao also says with a smile.

跨学科学习 Project

了解文房四宝，用毛笔写字
Learn the four Chinese treasures of the study and write with a Chinese writing brush

文化 Cultures

中西方绘画风格
Chinese and Western paintings

参考答案：
1 Yes, I do./No, I do not. They are just stories.
2 Yes, I believe there is./No, I do not think so. But I really wish there were such a thing as a magic pen.
3 I would draw a dog, because I want a pet./I would draw many trees and flowers to make the earth a better place to live.

Get ready

1 Do you think fairy tales can become real?

2 Is there a real magic pen?

3 What would you draw if you had a magic pen?

故事大意：
浩浩白天画了一只恐龙，结果晚上睡得迷迷糊糊间突然看见房间里出现了一只恐龙，他还以为自己画的画变成了真的。最后发现原来这是爸爸跟自己开的一个小玩笑。

běn zi
本子

qiān bǐ
铅笔

浩浩用铅笔在本子上画恐龙。

参考问题和答案：

1 What is Hao Hao doing? (He is drawing a dinosaur in a notebook with a pencil.)

2 What is Hao Hao thinking about? (He is imagining his drawing of a dinosa coming to life.)

3 Dad seems to have a good idea. Can you guess what it is? (He is going to take Ho Hao to a dinosaur museum./He is going to buy Hao Hao a dinosaur toy.)

zhǐ
纸

晚上，纸上的恐龙变成真的。

参考问题和答案：

1 What is Hao Hao doing? (He is sleeping.)
2 What is at the door? (A dinosaur.)
3 Is it a real dinosaur? (No, it is actually Dad in a dinosaur costume.)

wén jù hé
文具盒

"文具盒"也
可以叫"铅笔盒"。

参考问题和答案:
1 What is the 'dinosaur' doing? (It is opening Hao Hao's pencil case.)
2 What wakes Hao Hao up? (The sound of the pencil and the rubber falling onto the floor.)

xiàng pí
橡皮

恐龙打开文具盒，铅笔
和橡皮掉到地上。

chǐ zi
尺子

浩浩用尺子指向它，大叫："回去！"

参考问题和答案：

Why is Hao Hao holding a ruler? (Because he thinks that the dinosaur he drew on the paper has come to life. He is trying to force 'it' back to the paper.)

"是我啊，我是纸恐龙啊！"爸爸笑着说。

参考问题和答案：

Why is Hao Hao laughing? (Because he realized that the 'dinosaur' is Dad.)

"我也有一支神奇的笔！"
浩浩也笑着说。

参考问题和答案：
Hao Hao says that he has a magic pen as well. Why does he say that? (He is joking. Dad put on a dinosaur costume and went into his room. This makes it seem like Hao Hao's drawing has come to life.)

Let's think

1 Match and retell the story.

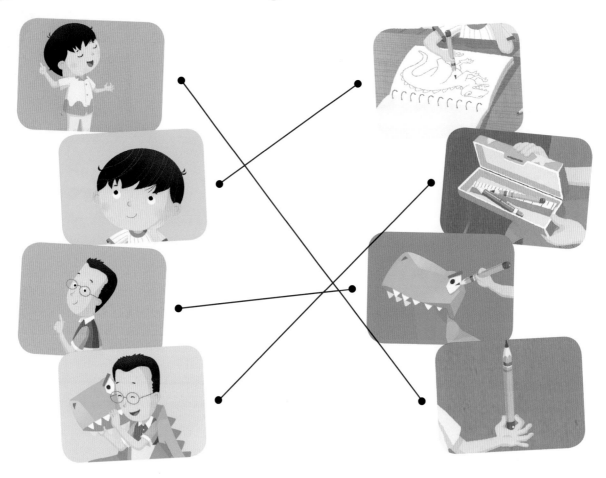

2 Design and draw a magic pen. Talk about it with your friend.

提醒学生可以赋予自己的神笔不同的功能，如：能治病、指地图上的地点人就可以到达那里、让人隐形等。

New words

1 Learn the new words.

恐龙　　笔　　铅笔　尺子　橡皮

用

本子　　文具盒　　纸

也

2 Look at the picture above and circle the correct answers.

a What stationery items can you see?

（铅笔）　恐龙　蛋糕　（橡皮）

b What does Hao Hao want to buy?

本子　　纸　　文具盒　（恐龙）

c Ling Ling also wants to buy a dinosaur.
Which character means 'also'?

（也）　不　是　有

第一题录音稿：

1 浩浩用铅笔在本子上画画。
2 文具盒里有尺子、铅笔、橡⋯
3 浩浩画了爸爸的眼睛和耳朵⋯
4 玲玲也喜欢画画，她画了"⋯恐龙爸爸"。

🎧 03 **1** Listen and circle the correct answers.

1 What is Hao Hao doing?

a 看书
(b) 画画
c 喝果汁

2 What is in the pencil case?

(a) 尺子
b 本子
c 文具盒

3 What did Hao Hao draw?

a 头
b 鼻子
(c) 耳朵

4 What did Ling Ling draw?

a 恐龙
(b) 爸爸
c 妈妈

🎧 04 **2** Look at the pictures. Listen to the st⋯

第二题参考问题和答案：

1 What are Ethan and Ivan drawing?
(They are drawing dinosaurs.)

2 What do you like to draw most? (I like
to draw cars/trees/animals most.)

可供替换的文具：纸、笔、橡皮、尺子、本子。
可供替换的颜色：黄、蓝、绿、黑、白、灰。

...nd say.

3 Role-play the dialogue with
your friend. Then replace
the red words with other
words and say.

你好。

你好。

有铅笔吗？

有。你喜欢什么颜色？

我喜欢红色的。

有文具盒吗？在哪里？

也有，在这里。

谢谢。

用什么笔画？

用铅笔画在纸上。

④

有尺子吗？

也有。

Task

Check if you have the same stationery as your friend. Complete the table and say.

我有蓝色的本子。

我也有。

我有红色的铅笔。

我没有。

	尺子	铅笔	文具盒	本子	纸
我也有					
我没有					

Game

Find out what you can put in the pencil case. Say in Chinese.

让学生先圈出所有可以放入文具盒内的物品，再逐一用中文说出它们的名称。

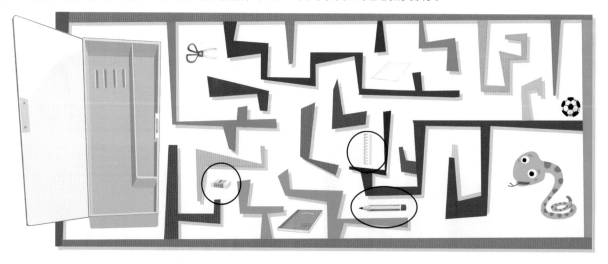

Song

学生一边唱歌，一边利用自己的文具配合歌词展示文具并做动作。

05 🎧 **Listen and sing.**

我的文具盒，

里面有什么？

铅笔直，尺子长，

用来做什么？

本子上写字，

白纸上画画，

还有橡皮一小块，

天天都用它。

课堂用语 Classroom language

安静一点。

Be quiet.

请注意。

Pay attention.

重要!

Important!

写一写 Write

1 Learn and trace the stroke. 老师示范笔画动作，学生跟着做：用手在空中画出"斜钩"。

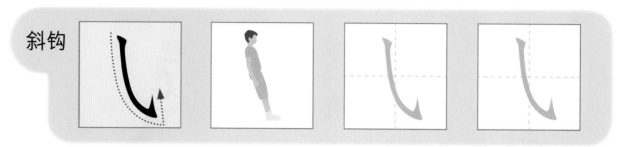

斜钩

2 Complete ⟍ in the following characters.

3 Find the strokes and trace them with the given colours.

撇折	提	撇	竖钩
			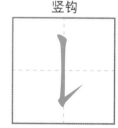
			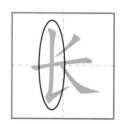

笔画"提"在"浩"和"现"、"撇"在"你"和"看"里的写法稍有差别。

4 Trace and write the character.

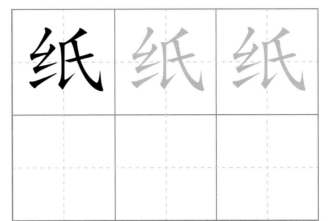

5 Write and say.

我们在 上画画。

汉字小常识 Did you know?

Many characters are made up of upper, middle and lower components.

Colour the upper component red, the middle component blue and the lower component green.

红色
蓝色
绿色

红色
蓝色
绿色

红色
蓝色
绿色

红色
蓝色
绿色

该结构中不同的字的上中下三个部件所占比例不一定相同。

多元学习 Connections

Cultures

中国画通常以毛笔作画，按题材主要分山水、花鸟和人物画。

1 Chinese and Western paintings have different styles. How do you like them? 问问学生这两组画他们比较喜欢哪一组，原因是什么。

Chinese painting is one of the oldest art forms in the world. It is done on rice paper or silk with black ink or coloured pigments.

Oil painting is very popular in Western countries. These paintings are done on canvas with oil paint.

2 Play a bingo game.

Find three animals painted in the same style in one straight line and say their names in Chinese.

这三张画都是中国画。

文房四宝（笔、墨、纸、砚）是中国古代传统的文房用具。"笔"指毛笔，笔头通常用动物毛制作。"墨"指墨条，是书写、绘画的颜料。"纸"指宣纸，是中国传统书画用纸。"砚"指砚台，用以磨墨，因为墨条需要加水研磨才能生成墨汁。

1 Do you know the Chinese four treasures of the study? Learn about their functions.

毛笔
Chinese writing brush

墨水
Ink

纸
Paper

砚台
Ink stone

2 Write Chinese calligraphy with the four treasures of the study and say.

我用毛笔在纸上写字。
我也有一支神奇的笔！

在课前准备几副笔、墨、纸、砚（或可用墨水代替墨条和砚台），让学生在课堂上使用。学生先参考小图学习正确握笔姿势，再试着写字。

游戏方法:

学生两人一组,先用橡皮制作简易骰子(两面写"1",两面写"2",最后两面写"3"),然后从第1格开始,两人轮流投掷并在转盘上前进相应步数,再回答停留的方格内的问题。看谁最快到达终点(第12格),同时回答问题又快又准。

1 Throw the dice with your friends and see who can finish the game first.

3 Write 'paper' in Chinese.

纸

4 你喜欢恐龙吗?
我喜欢/不喜欢恐龙。

2 Miss a turn.

5 尺子

1 这是什么?
文具盒

我喜欢尺子/铅笔/……

6 你喜欢什么文具?

12 Say 'I draw with a pencil.' in Chinese.

我用铅笔画画。

这是本子。

7 这是什么?

11 你有几支铅笔?
我有一/二/……支铅笔。

8 你的文具盒里有什么?
我的文具盒里有铅笔、橡皮、……

10 Say 'I also have a magic pen.' in Chinese.
我也有一支神奇的笔。

橡皮

9

2 **Work with your friend. Colour the stars and the chillies.**

Words	说	读	写
也	☆	☆	🌶
纸	☆	☆	☆
笔	☆	☆	🌶
铅笔	☆	☆	🌶
橡皮	☆	☆	🌶
尺子	☆	☆	🌶
本子	☆	☆	🌶
文具盒	☆	☆	🌶

Words and sentences	说	读	写
用	☆	🌶	🌶
恐龙	☆	🌶	🌶
我也有一支神奇的笔。	☆	🌶	🌶
浩浩也笑着说。	☆	🌶	🌶

Say the names of some stationery items	☆

3 **What does your teacher say?**

My teacher says ...

21

分享 Sharing

Words I remember

也	yě	also, as well
纸	zhǐ	paper
笔	bǐ	pen
铅笔	qiān bǐ	pencil
橡皮	xiàng pí	rubber
尺子	chǐ zi	ruler
本子	běn zi	notebook
文具盒	wén jù hé	pencil case
用	yòng	to use
恐龙	kǒng lóng	dinosaur

Other words

神奇	shén qí	magical
变成	biàn chéng	to become
真的	zhēn de	real
打开	dǎ kāi	to open
掉	diào	to drop
地	dì	floor
指向	zhǐ xiàng	to point at
回去	huí qù	to go back
笑	xiào	to smile
说	shuō	to say
支	zhī	(measure word for pens)
啊	a	(a particle used at the end of a sentence to express appreciation or indicate a pause)

延伸活动：
1 学生用手遮盖英文，读中文单词，并思考单词意思；
2 学生用手遮盖中文单词，看着英文说出对应的中文单词；
3 学生三人一组，尽量运用中文单词分角色复述故事。

OXFORD
UNIVERSITY PRESS

Oxford University Press is a department of the University of Oxford.
It furthers the University's objective of excellence in research, scholarship,
and education by publishing worldwide. Oxford is a registered trade mark of
Oxford University Press in the UK and in certain other countries

Published in Hong Kong by
Oxford University Press (China) Limited
39th Floor, One Kowloon, 1 Wang Yuen Street, Kowloon Bay,
Hong Kong

© Oxford University Press (China) Limited 2017

The moral rights of the author have been asserted

First Edition published in 2017

Illustrated by Anne Lee, Wildman, KY Chan and KK Ng

Photographs for reproduction permitted by Dreamstime.com

China National Publications Import & Export (Group) Corporation is an authorized distributor of
Oxford Elementary Chinese.

Please contact content@cnpiec.com.cn or 86-10-65856782

ISBN: 978-0-19-082195-1

10 9 8 7 6 5 4 3

Teacher's Edition
ISBN: 978-0-19-082207-1

10 9 8 7 6 5 4 3 2